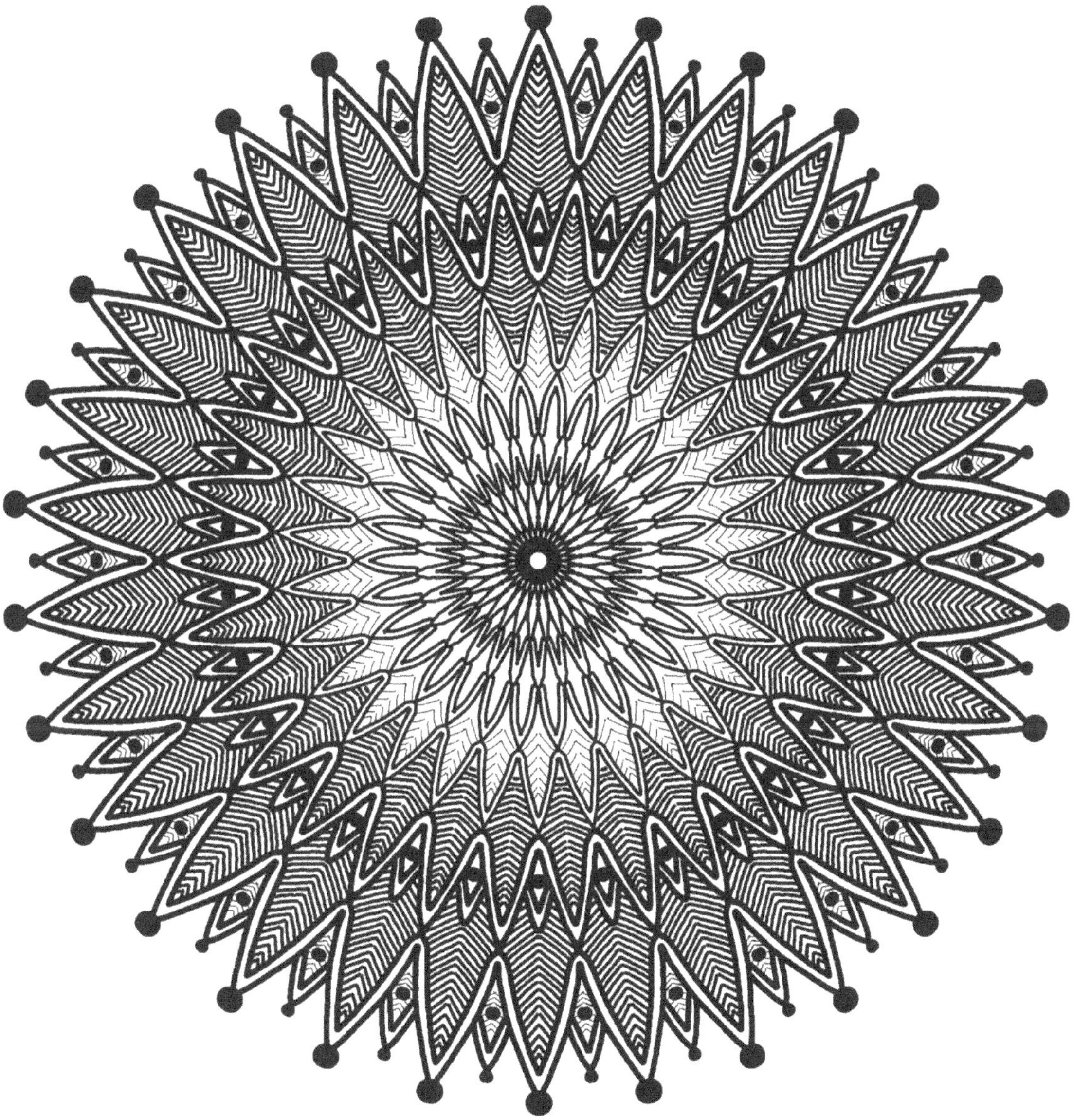

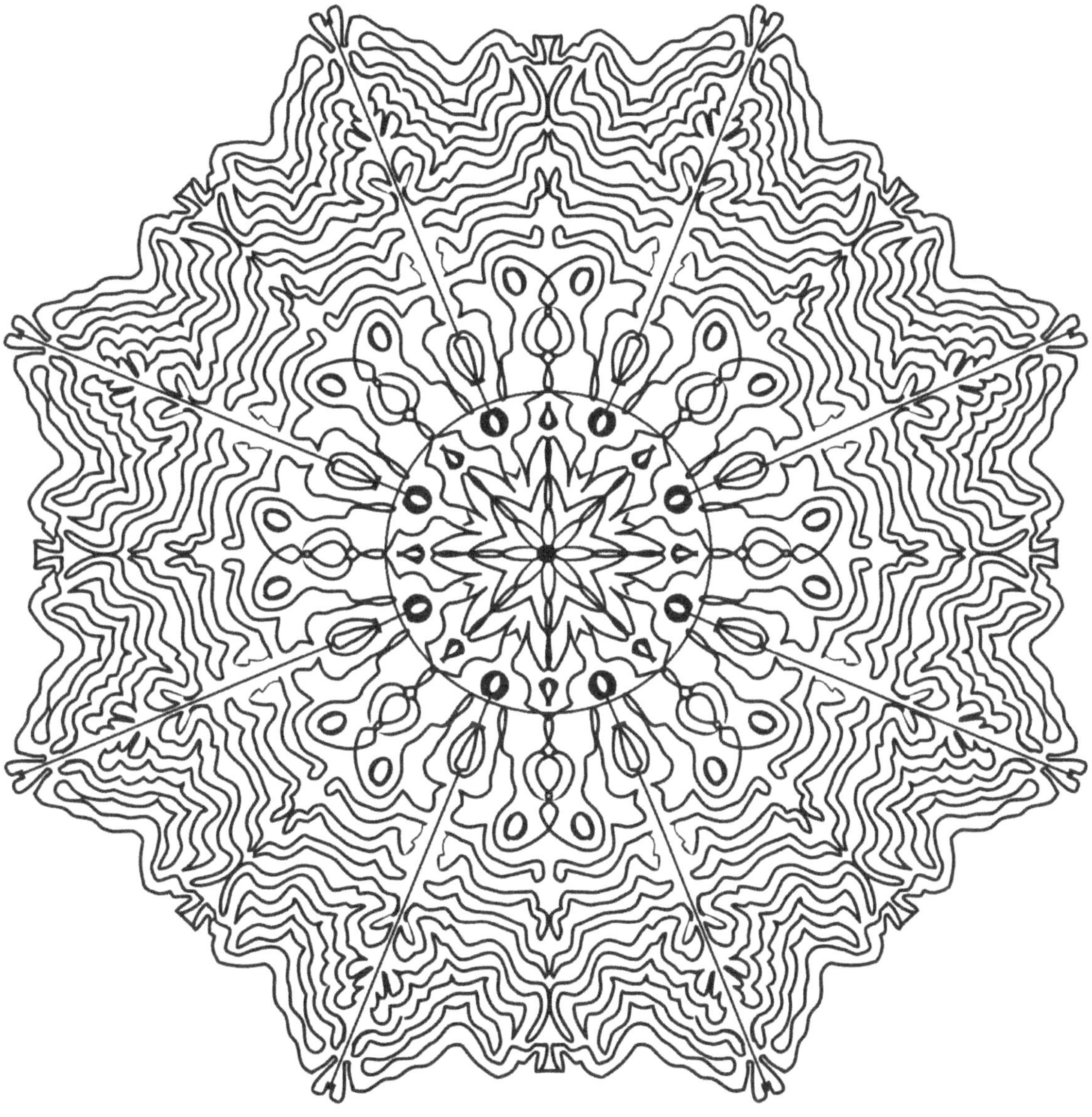

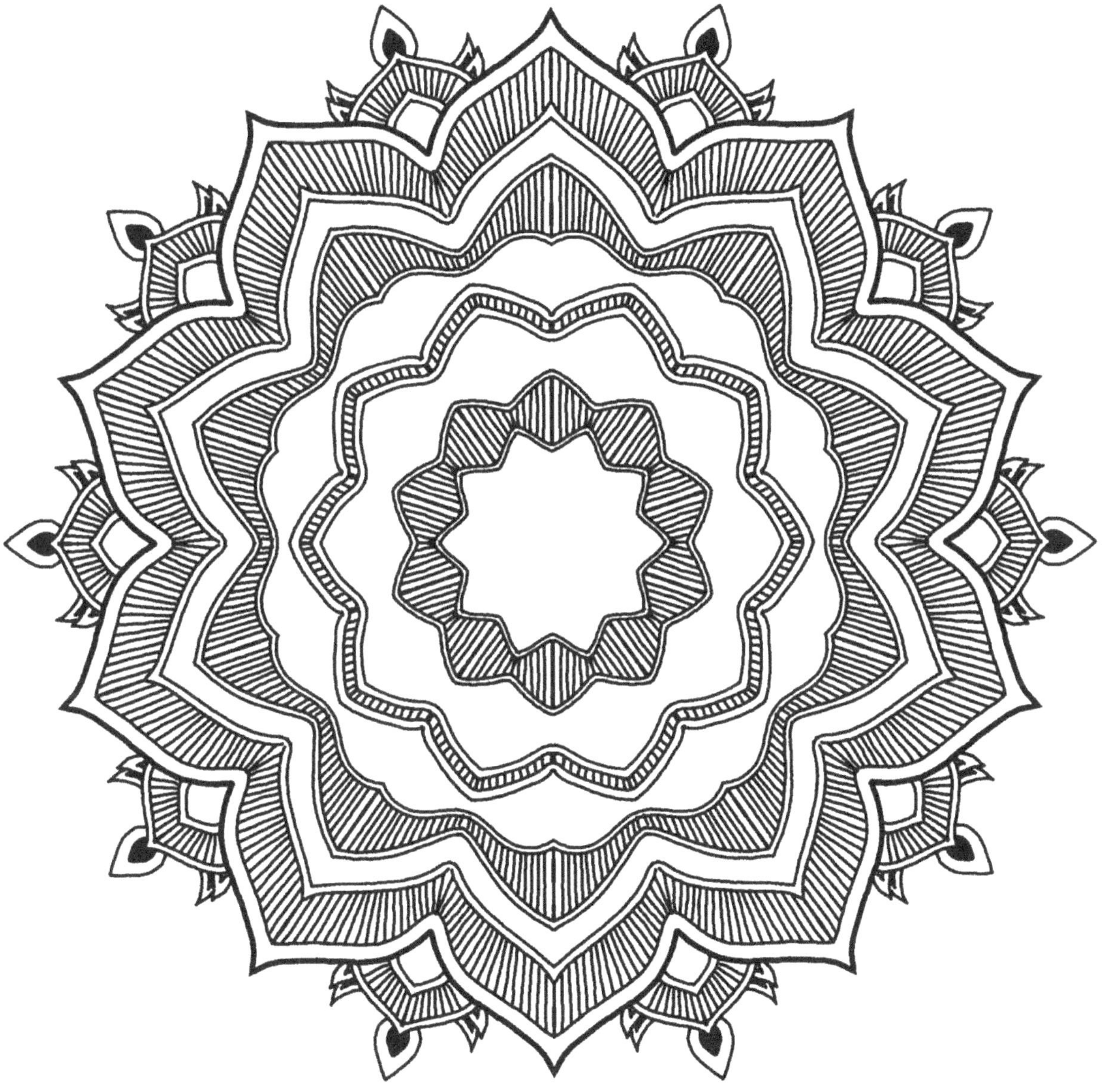

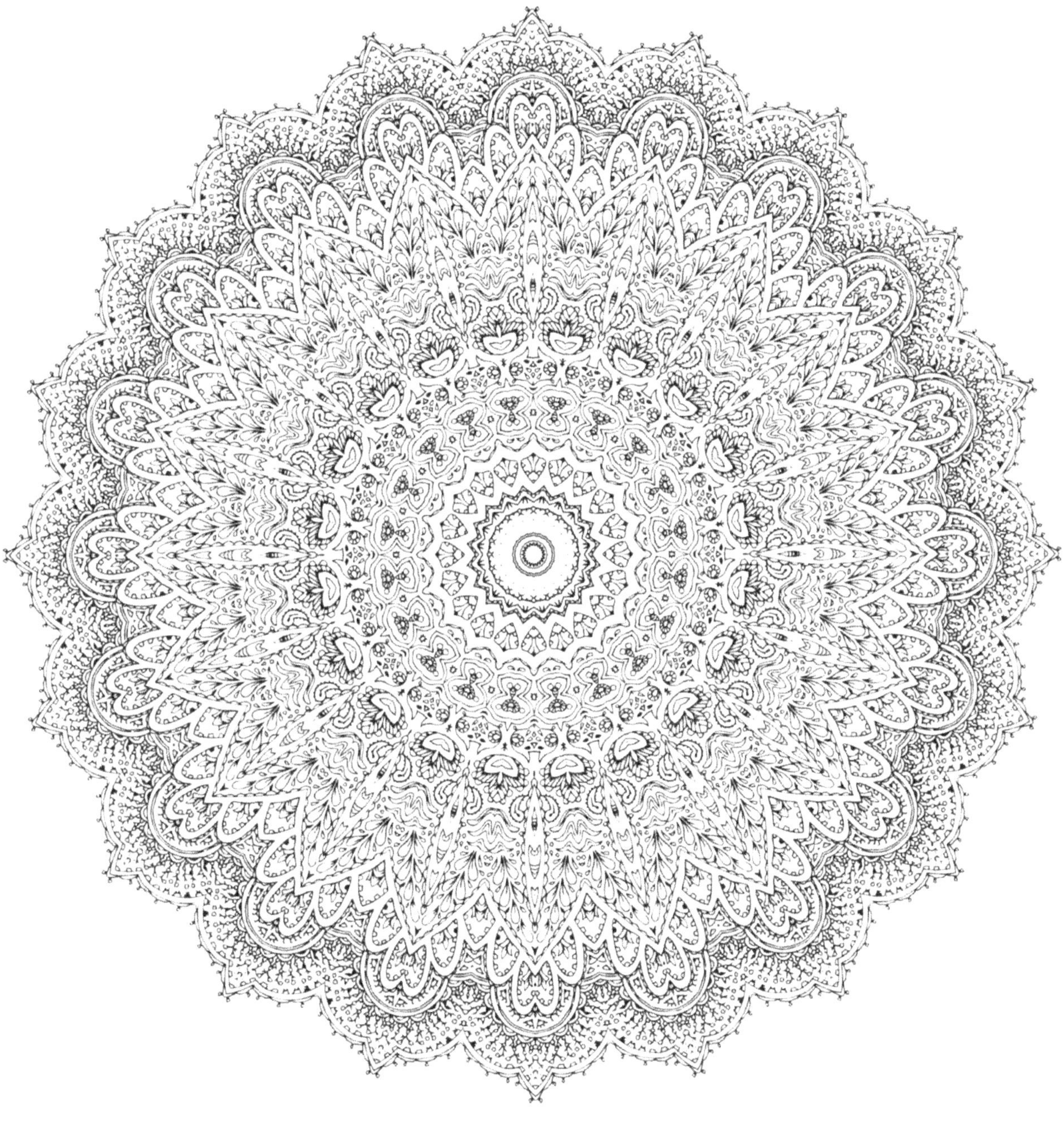

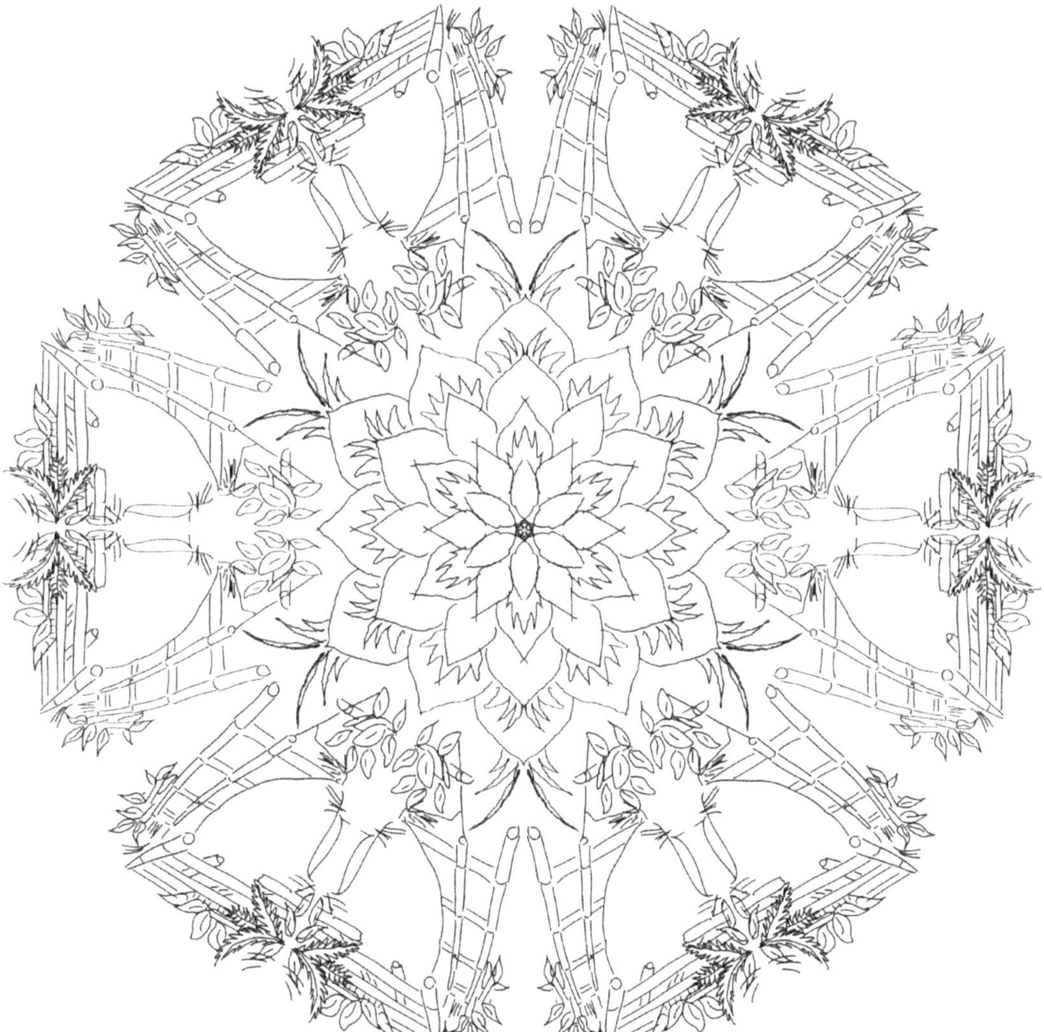

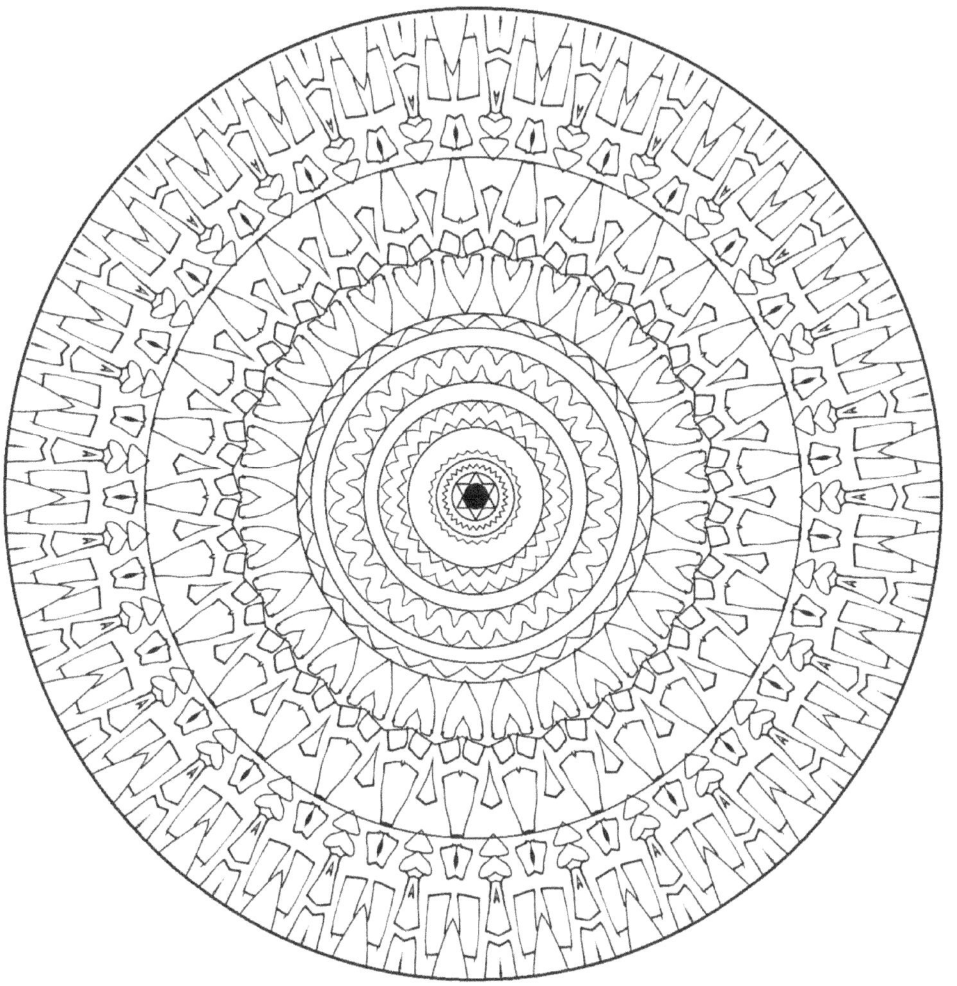

La Princesse Company

Visit us at: Ordercoloringbook.com

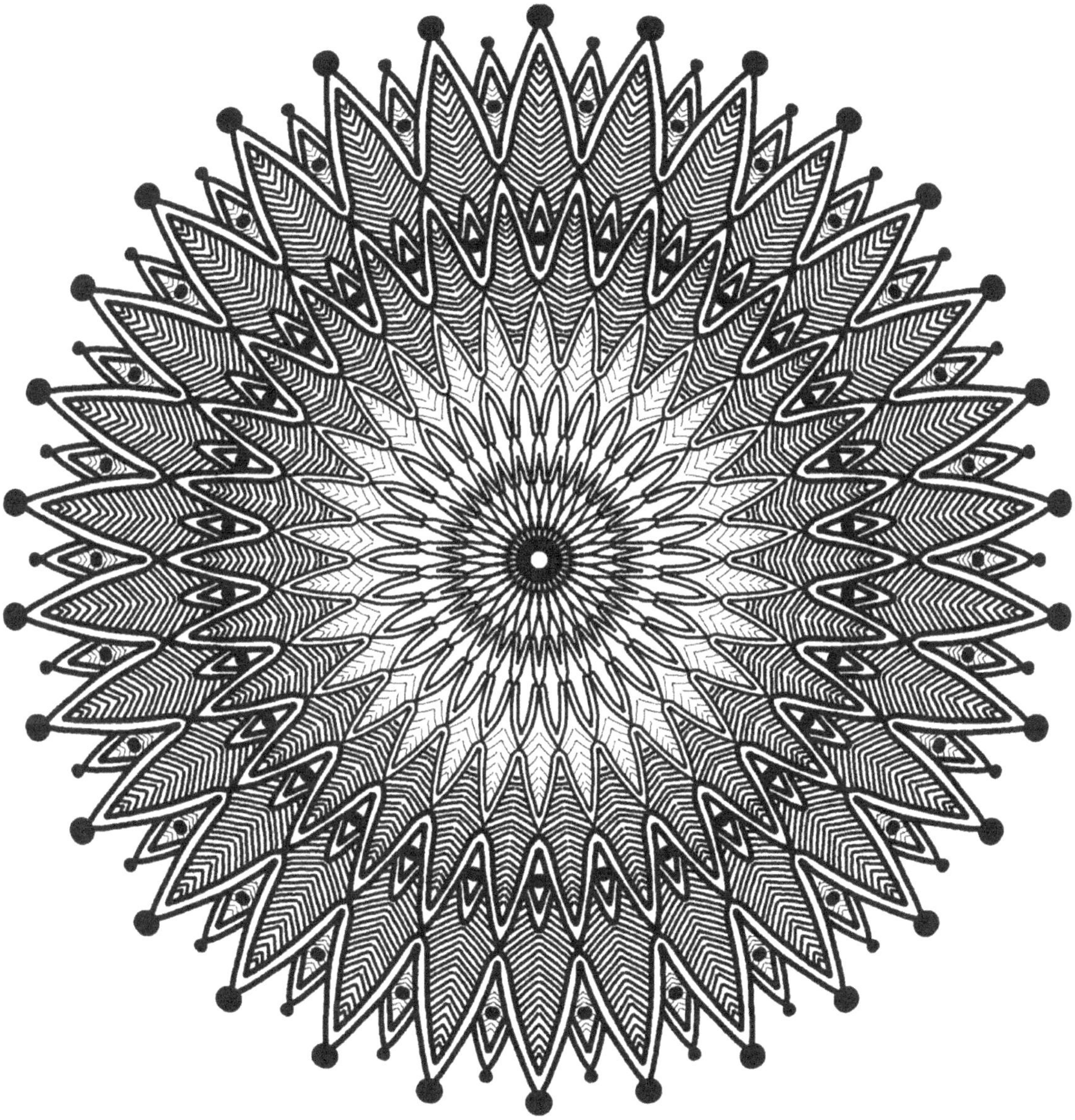

www.ingramcontent.com/pod-product-compliance
Lightning Source LLC
Chambersburg PA
CBHW082333220526
45470CB00008B/2498
* 9 7 8 1 9 7 9 8 2 3 7 1 5 *